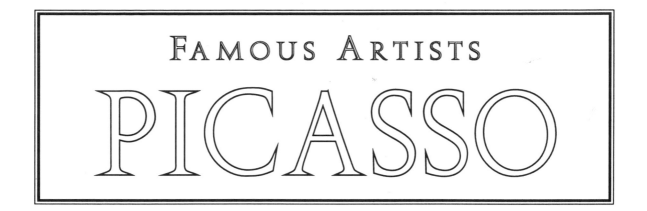

FAMOUS ARTISTS

PICASSO

The author, Antony Mason, is a freelance editor and author of
many books for children.

Designer	Peter Bennett
Editor	Sarah Levete
Picture research	Brooks-Krikler Research
Illustrator	Michaela Stewart
Collages	Peter Bennett

First edition for the United States, Canada, and the Philippines
published 1995 by Barron's Educational Series, Inc.

Designed and produced by
Aladdin Books Ltd
28 Percy Street
London W1P 9FF

First published in
Great Britain in 1994 by
Watts Books
96 Leonard Street
London EC2A 4RH

All inquiries should be addressed to:
Barron's Educational Series, Inc.
250 Wireless Boulevard
Hauppauge, New York 11788

Library of Congress Catalog Card No.: 94-79547

International Standard Book No. 0-8120-6496-8 (hardcover)
0-8120-9175-2 (paperback)

Printed in Belgium
4567 4208 9876543

FAMOUS ARTISTS

PICASSO

ANTONY MASON

BARRON'S

CONTENTS

Two Women on the Beach, painted in 1956.

INTRODUCTION

Pablo Picasso (1881–1973) is considered by many to be the greatest artist of the twentieth century. Picasso was at the forefront of the development of modern art. With fellow artist Georges Braque, he founded the revolutionary art movement known as Cubism. His restless energy took him in many new directions. Rejecting conventional approaches to art, Picasso brought a new sense of freedom to both painting and sculpture. He was an attractive and unpredictable character, dedicated to art and to discovering new forms of expression. This book explores Picasso's development, from his childhood in Spain, during which he showed remarkable gifts for drawing and painting, to his old age in the south of France. It discusses the techniques that he used to create his major works — and also shows you how you can try out some of these for yourself. Below you can see how the book is organized.

Illustration of
the artist's home or
environment

The story of
the artist's life

An enlargement of part
of the painting

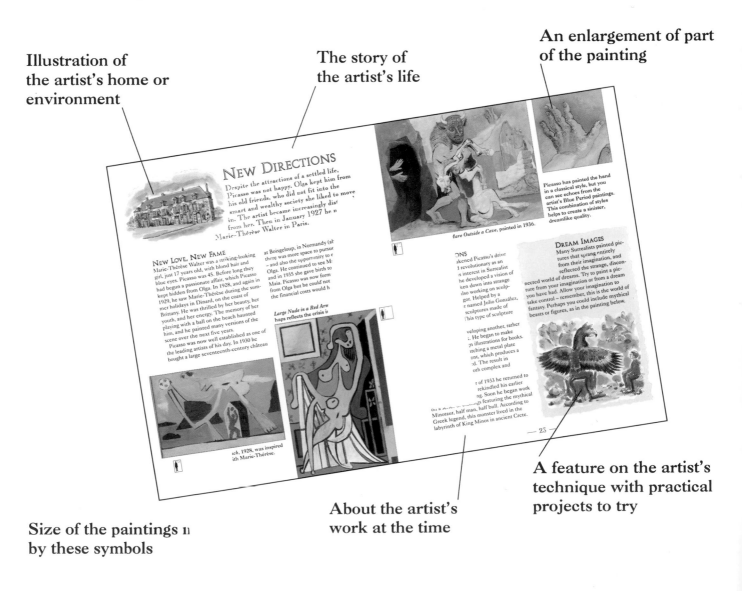

A feature on the artist's
technique with practical
projects to try

About the artist's
work at the time

Size of the paintings
by these symbols

THE GIFTED CHILD

Born into an artistic family, it is said that Pablo Picasso could draw before he could talk. His first teacher was his father, José, who encouraged his young son's talent. He attended art schools in Barcelona and Madrid. Even at the age of 18, Picasso was beginning to challenge accepted wisdom about art, and was making friends with leading young artists and writers.

EARLY SIGNS OF GREATNESS

Pablo Ruiz Picasso was born in Málaga, in southern Spain, on October 25, 1881. He was the son of a painter and art teacher named José Ruiz Blasco. His mother was named María Picasso Lopez, and in the Spanish tradition Pablo bore both his parents' names. Picasso spent his first years in Málaga, living in the house (above) where his two younger sisters were also born. In 1891 the family moved to La Coruña in northern Spain, where his father took a job as an art teacher. Picasso was already showing a remarkable talent for drawing and painting.

His family was not happy in La Coruña, and they were devastated when Picasso's younger sister Conchita died of diphtheria. In 1895 they moved to Barcelona, capital of the Catalania region of Spain, where Picasso, only age 14, attended the School of Fine Arts. There he demonstrated his skill, completing tasks with exceptional speed. In 1897 Picasso's painting *Science and Charity* received special acclaim at a national exhibition held in Madrid. The realistic scene was painted with great confidence and technical ability for a boy just 16 years old. After this success Picasso attended the Royal Academy of San Fernando in Madrid, but he left after a few months.

Back in the lively city of Barcelona he fell in with a group of artists who met at a café called Els Quatre Gats (The Four Cats). He shared a flat with a fellow painter named Carlos Casagemas, and they lived in happy poverty. They were so poor that Picasso painted furniture and bookcases on the walls of the flat to make it look furnished.

An early self-portrait, 1896, shows Picasso as he saw himself at age 15.

A Freer Style

Picasso painted and drew with great energy from an early age, doing portraits of his family, landscapes, religious subjects, pictures of animals and bullfights, and studies of sculptures. At this time his work was classical and realistic, influenced by earlier Spanish masters, such as El Greco and Diego Velázquez, whom he had studied in Madrid.

In Barcelona, at Els Quatre Gats, Picasso began to take a freer approach to his work and showed a greater sense of design – the way in which the composition fits into the frame of the picture. He designed posters and menus to earn some extra money.

The young Picasso showed a talent for poster design. In this sketch for a poster he achieves a lively mood and sense of movement by using scratchy lines of black chalk and rapidly applying broad areas of paint.

In 1899 Picasso entered a competition to design a poster for a carnival.

Design a Poster

A poster needs to be eye-catching. Think about what image you can use that will best represent the product or event you want to advertise. Use a simple but striking design that will stand out. Keep it simple, but don't forget that you must include some written information as part of your composition – the time and place of an event, for example. Think carefully about the size and style of the lettering and how you can incorporate it into your design: does it fit in with the image you are trying to create? Use strong, bold colors to paint your poster.

PARIS

Picasso's first exhibition was held at Els Quatre Gats in 1900. One of his works was selected for the Spanish pavilion at the Exposition Universelle in Paris later that year. Paris was then the center of European art. Picasso and his friend and fellow painter Carlos Casagemas decided it was time to see Paris for themselves.

SUCCESS AND SADNESS

In Paris, Picasso was given a contract to produce a series of paintings. In spite of this success, he soon returned to Spain with Carlos Casagemas, who had become depressed over a love affair. Picasso began work in Madrid as editor and illustrator for a new magazine called *Arte Joven* (*Young Art*). Meanwhile the lovesick Casagemas had returned to Paris. In early 1901 Casagemas committed suicide.

Child Holding A Dove, painted in 1901.

This self-portrait painted in 1901 reflects Picasso's sorrow and poverty at the time.

Picasso was devastated by the death of his friend, and the mood of his painting became more reflective and somber. When *Arte Joven* failed, he returned to Barcelona, but in the spring of 1901 he went back to Paris. An art dealer, Ambroise Vollard, held an exhibition of his work there. It was a great success.

Picasso had proved that he was a naturally gifted draftsman (someone who can draw), but at the age of 20 he rejected the conventions of skilled drawing. Here the lines are bold and crude, and the color is laid on thickly with heavy brushstrokes.

The Harlequin and His Companion, 1901.

CREATING HIS OWN STYLE

Picasso was impressed by Paris – its lively artistic scene, the bohemian life in the artistic quarter of Montmartre, and the busy bars. At this time there was a major change in Picasso's work, with a more daring use of color. At first his work in Paris reflected the style of the painters he studied there. He painted street scenes in the Impressionist style, and broke up areas of color into bright dots, in the manner of the Pointillist Georges Seurat. Soon, however, Picasso was creating his own style, using strong outlines filled with areas of textured but flat color. Until this time, most painting had attempted to imitate three-dimensional reality; scenes had to look as though they had depth. Picasso was more interested in the emotions that painting could convey.

BALANCING COLORS

Have a look at the color wheel (below) to see how different colors work together. The six basic colors on the color wheel are divided into two groups. Red, yellow, and blue are the purest colors, also known as primary colors. The secondary colors, green, orange, and purple, are mixed from the two colors on either side.

Colors on opposite sides of the color wheel, for example green and red, are known as complementary colors. In his painting *The Harlequin and His Companion* (above), Picasso used a scheme of complementary colors. When placed side by side, these colors intensify one another.

Experiment with color-mixing yourself, using different combinations of primary and secondary colors. See what different tones you create. Experiment using complementary colors.

THE BLUE PERIOD

Picasso moved back and forth between Paris and Barcelona from 1901 until 1904. During this time he began to paint increasingly in shades of blue, and chose melancholy subjects — poverty, oppression, and loneliness. Picasso had found a distinctive style and voice. These paintings belong to what is known as Picasso's "Blue Period."

IMAGES OF SADNESS

The death of Casagemas triggered off a profound sadness in Picasso. Like many of his artistic friends, Picasso was living in poverty in a series of squalid flats and hotel rooms in run-down parts of Paris. In October 1902 he began sharing a flat in Paris with a French poet named Max Jacob. They could not even afford two beds. Picasso slept in the bed during the day, and Jacob, who had a day job as a tutor, slept in it at night. Through his friendship with Max Jacob, Picasso began to feel less of a foreigner in Paris – though he never lost his strong Spanish accent. Jacob was the first of many poets with whom Picasso became close friends at various points in his life.

When he could not even afford canvas and oil paint, Picasso concentrated on drawings. He sketched tramps, drunks, and blind beggars, and he used models from a women's prison in Paris. They often appear as portraits of mother-and-child, since the women were allowed to keep their infants in prison. These paintings were full of raw emotion. In 1903 Picasso returned to Barcelona, and in the next 14 months he completed 50 Blue Period paintings.

The Absinthe Drinker **was painted in 1901. Absinthe is a strong drink that is now illegal.**

Many of Picasso's paintings of this period include a small still life – often bottles and glasses depicted with their shine. This element of sharp focus in the foreground helps to balance the composition, and it also shows that the scene is a bar.

Compared to the rest of his body, the man's face is precisely painted, in shades of blue. This mixture of techniques and finishes in a single painting became a feature of Picasso's later painting.

LA VIE (LIFE)

Back in Barcelona, Picasso produced one of the largest and most effective of his Blue Period paintings. Called *La Vie (Life)*, it appears to show a naked artist and his lover, and a woman with a child. The artist's face is a portrait of Picasso's friend Casagemas, who had committed suicide over a failed love affair. It is a complex painting that can be interpreted on many levels. Perhaps it reflects Picasso's feelings about love and his deep sorrow at the death of Casagemas.

 La Vie, 1903, from Picasso's Blue Period, reflects a somber mood.

 ## PAINTING IN ONE COLOR

Painting with different shades of just one color can be very effective. This is called monochromatic painting. Try it for yourself. Choose a simple subject and make a quick sketch first. Create different shades of the same color by adding varying amounts of white paint (or water, if you are using water-color). Apply these shades carefully to show the three-dimensional nature of your subject. Use the darkest tone for the shadow and the lightest tone for the areas exposed to the most light.

The Rose Period

In 1904 Picasso moved back to Paris, and from this time on he lived almost continuously in France, returning rarely to his homeland. Picasso rented a studio in a run-down block of flats in Montmartre (left), which Max Jacob nicknamed the Bateau Lavoir (Floating Laundry). Here he met his first great love, a beautiful woman named Fernande Olivier.

Picasso was a lively and attractive man, but he became moody if his painting was not going well. He had many love affairs throughout his life, and his style of painting is often said to have changed every time he found a new partner. In the winter of 1904, after he had met Fernande Olivier, he introduced a greater range of color into his work, especially pink (*rose*, in French). His work from this time is known as his "Rose Period," which lasted until 1906.

Boy with a Pipe, 1905, has much warmer colors than Picasso's Blue Period work.

Blue tones dominate in *Woman in a Chemise*, 1905, from Picasso's Rose Period.

The Floating Laundry

Back in Paris, Picasso, now age 23, was happy in the company of a boisterous set of painters and poets living in the Floating Laundry. Although this was neither a laundry nor a boat, the name stuck. Few of his friends had any money, but they were fulfilled by their art and they enjoyed life. Picasso remained there for five years.

STUDIES IN PINK

In 1904 Picasso met the poet Guillaume Apollinaire, and together they developed an interest in the world of circus performers and actors. Acrobats and the clownlike character Harlequin became the subject for many of Picasso's new paintings. They were usually portrayed at rest, looking reflective and silent. By 1906 Picasso was experimenting with pictures painted entirely in pink tones. He made a series of paintings and drawings of boys and horses. But Picasso was always restless, looking for new ways to express himself. His style of painting never stayed the same for long.

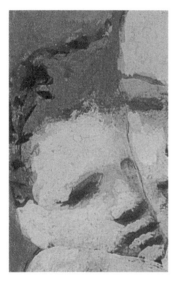

Picasso made a number of studies of boys when he was staying in Gôsol, in the Spanish Pyrenees. The style is typical of the artist at this time. He uses simplified shapes and only minimal detail. The simplicity of the work creates a sense of innocence and honesty.

 The Two Brothers, painted in 1906, has a timeless, classical quality.

BODY PROPORTIONS

The shape of the human body changes gradually from infancy to adulthood. The head of a baby is large compared to the rest of its body; a child's shape is rounded compared to the more muscular and elongated form of an adult. Use the picture on the right as a guide. Now try studying and sketching people of different ages. How long is your model's neck? How big are the hands compared to the face? Where do the arms reach down to? Check these constantly as you draw.

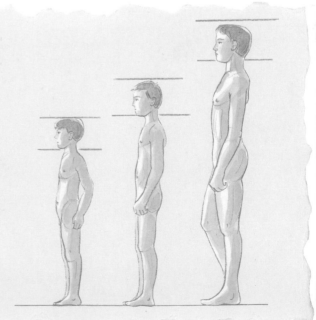

CONTROVERSY

During his travels in Spain in 1906, Picasso saw many examples of ancient and early Christian sculptures. He was struck by their power and the immediacy of their expression. This was the beginning of Picasso's interest in non-European and "primitive" art. Back in Paris his painting took an entirely new course.

AFRICAN INFLUENCES

Picasso's interest in ancient sculpture soon led him to study African art in the museums of Paris. He was fascinated by the way in which African sculpture distorted the human body into imaginative and original shapes. Picasso now began to use brighter colors. He was influenced by two contemporary artists, Paul Cézanne and Paul Gauguin, who had developed their own styles of painting. Cézanne broke up the world into flat, geometric shapes, and Gauguin's sculpture had been strongly influenced by the art of the Polynesian islands.

Picasso left the Rose Period behind him and began a new experimental phase. He concentrated on one large canvas, *Les Demoiselles d'Avignon (The Girls of Avignon)*. This painting represents a turning point in the history of modern art.

Picasso made hundreds of preparatory drawings for *Les Demoiselles d'Avignon*. The canvas took many months to complete, for the artist was always returning to it to introduce new ideas and styles. The two figures on the right were reworked after the artist had left the canvas for several months, to reflect Picasso's growing interest in African art.

This controversial and radical painting broke with the traditional representation of the nude, and provoked hostile criticism. Many people did not understand or like Picasso's new work. But the artist enjoyed being the center of controversy. He continued to work in this innovative direction.

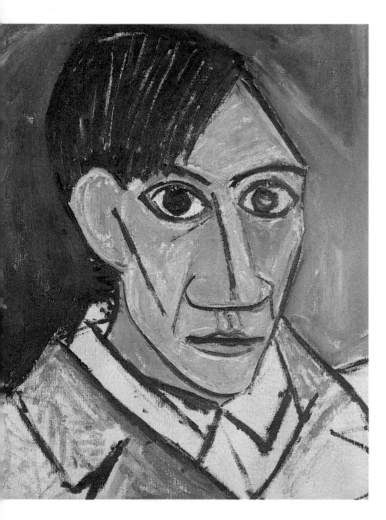

This self-portrait, 1907, shows the new direction of Picasso's work.

Some of the faces and limbs have been bizarrely distorted. Others have been reduced to geometric shapes. The mysterious and powerful masklike faces of the figures on the right reflect clearly the influence of African art on Picasso's work.

The controversial *Les Demoiselles d'Avignon*, 1907.

BREAKING WITH THE PAST
Les Demoiselles d'Avignon is sometimes called the first masterpiece of twentieth-century art. No one had ever painted like this before. Instead of representing a scene as it might exist in reality, Picasso broke it up into a series of planes and colors. He suddenly discovered all kinds of new possibilities for painting opening up before him.

EXPRESSING YOURSELF
How do you see your subject? As an artist, how can you best convey your vision? You may be able to convey the essence of your subject better by departing from conventional ideas of perspective. You may feel that unusual and unexpected colors are needed to convey your vision. Feel free to experiment. Play around with shape, tone, and texture, perhaps introducing dots, streaks, or patches of color. The effects can be very dramatic.

CUBISM

In 1907 Picasso met a French artist called Georges Braque. When they met again the following year they realized that they had both been pursuing similar ideas: they were breaking up their compositions into geometric shapes, to show the subject from more than one angle at a time. Working together closely, they forged a revolutionary style of painting that soon became known as Cubism.

A Cubist portrait of Ambroise Vollard, the celebrated art dealer, painted in 1910.

RADICAL CHANGES

With Cubism, Picasso had embarked on yet another challenging and experimental path. This new style was a complete break with traditional ideas of perspective and the representation of the human form. At first, art critics were shocked by the new movement. They had never seen anything like this before. Soon, however, hostility turned to admiration.

A critic first coined the term "Cubist" although the paintings of Braque and Picasso at this time did more than break the world up into cubes. They broke it up into a complex series of planes, interleaved and delicately shaded in a limited range of colors.

In another pioneering move, Picasso began to add lettering to his work. In 1911, he wrote the words "Ma Jolie" (My Pretty One) on a painting. This was the name of a song – but it was also probably a reference to the new woman who had entered his life, Eva Gouel Humbert.

Picasso was widely respected for his innovative work. Now a successful artist, Picasso left the Floating Laundry and moved into a larger flat in a smart part of Paris, Montparnasse. He soon abandoned Fernande Olivier for his new love, Eva.

Taken out of context, this face is only just recognizable, although it is possible to identify eyes, nose, and mouth. Picasso often used somber colors for these paintings – gray, brown, ocher, and blue. The shadowy effect gives the painting a sense of mystery and timelessness.

Seated Nude, 1909-10, shows the human form reassembled as a series of flat planes.

SEEING ALL ANGLES

In Cubism the artist presents the subject from several sides at once. See how this works by using paper cutouts. Find a magazine that has several pictures of the same subject – a fashion model or sports event, perhaps. Cut out the images. Mix them up and rearrange them on a piece of paper. Experiment with the pieces at different angles until you arrive at the composition you like most. How does your picture differ from the original subject?

PUSHING REALITY TO THE LIMITS

Picasso and Braque made no attempt to paint the subject as it really was. "I paint objects as I think them, not as I see them," said Picasso. Cubism was an intellectual exercise, a way of looking at the world to see how it could be reshaped. What began as a portrait of someone or an object such as a guitar, became a design in its own right. All the surfaces and shadows were fractured and reshaped so that the final image was only distantly related to the original subject. But Picasso was quick to point out that his works still represented something, however vaguely. "There is no abstract art," he said. "You must always start with something. Afterwards you can remove all traces of reality."

SYNTHETIC CUBISM

The first period of Cubism, from 1909 to 1912, is referred to as Analytical Cubism, because the artists were analyzing what they saw and reinterpreting its structure. In 1912, however, Picasso and Braque began to stick objects and pieces of material onto their work. This period is called Synthetic Cubism.

MOUNTAINEERS IN ART

During the first phase of Cubism, Braque and Picasso had created works by breaking down reality into a series of geometric planes. Now they created work by building it

out of objects they had found. At first they used images of flat objects in their work, such as chair caning or newspaper lettering, painting them so precisely that they looked real. Soon they began to use actual objects, sticking pieces of sandpaper, wallpaper, and newspaper onto their paintings. It was the first time that the technique of collage had been used in modern art. The style of their painting also changed. It was often little more than a series of geometric lines on a white background, with some planes of color. Objects were reduced to simple symbols – for example, a guitar might be represented by two wavy lines.

Picasso and Braque continued to collaborate closely – "roped together as mountaineers," as Braque said. They became good friends, and vacationed together in the south of France. In 1914, however, World War I broke out, and Braque joined the French army in order to fight against the Germans. The mood of Europe changed radically. The pioneering age of Cubism had come to an end.

 Portrait of a Young Girl, painted in 1914, shows the brighter colors used by Picasso.

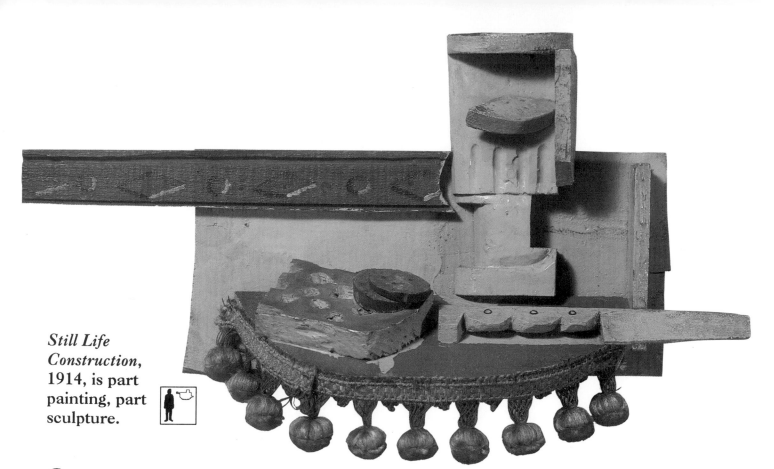

Still Life Construction, 1914, is part painting, part sculpture.

CONSTRUCTIONS

Since 1906 Picasso had shown a great interest in sculpture. However, he kept his sculpture hidden from public view, and few people knew about this side of his work until the 1960s.

Like his painting, Picasso's sculpture was highly experimental. During this time he constructed sculptures out of various materials and found objects, such as sheets of metal, tin cans, and spoons. This had never been done before. Picasso also painted many of his sculptures. In this way he played with the traditional differences that separate painting from sculpture. His paintings became rather like sculptures, and his sculptures became rather like paintings.

COLLAGE

Collage is a simple, but exciting way in which to construct images. You will need glue and an assortment of everyday objects and materials – for example, newspapers, cloth, tissue paper, sandpaper, tinfoil, bottle tops, grasses, and leaves. Use them to construct a scene. You could use sandpaper to represent a beach, blue cloth as the sea, cutouts of paper for sailing boats, and green paper for the distant hills. Invent your own original image, a mixture of geometric shapes and recognizable objects – as Picasso would have done.

WORLD WAR I

Picasso remained in Paris for most of the war. These were depressing times. Many of his friends were involved in the fighting or had left the city. At the end of 1915, Picasso's beloved companion, Eva, died suddenly of tuberculosis. Picasso was devastated. Then in 1917 his life took a new turn.

PARADE

Picasso was invited by his friend, the innovative playwright and poet Jean Cocteau, to design the sets and costumes for a new ballet called *Parade*. This was a major cultural event, involving leading figures in contemporary music, literature, and dance. Picasso designed Cubist scenery and extravagant, sculptural costumes. When the ballet was first performed in Paris, it was not well received. In fact, it caused an uproar.

However, during the rehearsals in Rome (above left) for the ballet, Picasso had become entranced by a beautiful dancer named Olga Kokhlova. They were married in 1918, and in 1921 Olga gave birth to a son, Paulo. They led a grand life. For a while, Picasso's life seemed successful and stable, and his paintings had a brighter, sunnier feel.

Portrait of Olga in an Armchair, 1917, shows Picasso returning to a more classical style.

Mother and Son, 1921, was inspired by Paulo's birth.

PAINTING THE SUBCONSCIOUS

During this time, Picasso worked in a variety of styles simultaneously. Some of his work seemed traditional, but he did not abandon Cubism altogether. In 1925 Picasso became closely involved with a group of writers and artists who called themselves Surrealists. They were interested in the world of the subconscious – the world of dreams and spontaneous behavior. At this time Picasso produced *The Three Dancers*, a dreamlike picture. The painting is ambiguous – is it a joyful dance, or is it a crucifixion?

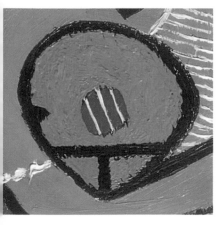

Picasso has combined a mixture of styles and finishes. The painting has Cubist elements but by using brighter colors and with imaginative content, Picasso has created something quite fresh and new.

The Three Dancers, 1925, marks a new direction in Picasso's career.

SKETCHING

As you can see from Picasso's drawing (left) and the sketch on the right, a portrait does not need to be a finished painting. It can be a free, lively sketch. Loosen up your sketching by trying the following techniques. First, do a drawing of someone without looking at your paper at all. Then try to sketch someone without lifting your pencil from the paper. You could work from life or from a photograph, as Picasso did when he painted the portrait of Olga (opposite page). You could do a series of sketches of the same subject from different angles. Why not choose the one you like most and use that position for a more detailed portrait painting?

NEW DIRECTIONS

Despite the attractions of a settled life, Picasso was not happy. Olga kept him from his old friends, who did not fit into the smart and wealthy society she liked to move in. The artist became increasingly distanced from her. Then in January 1927 he met Marie-Thérèse Walter in Paris.

NEW LOVE, NEW FAME

Marie-Thérèse Walter was a striking-looking girl, just 17 years old, with blond hair and blue eyes. Picasso was 45. Before long they had begun a passionate affair, which Picasso kept hidden from Olga. In 1928, and again in 1929, he saw Marie-Thérèse during the summer holidays in Dinard, on the coast of Brittany. He was thrilled by her beauty, her youth, and her energy. The memory of her playing with a ball on the beach haunted him, and he painted many versions of the scene over the next five years.

Picasso was now well established as one of the leading artists of his day. In 1930 he bought a large seventeenth-century château at Boisgeloup, in Normandy (above), where there was more space to pursue his sculpture – and also the opportunity to escape from Olga. He continued to see Marie-Thérèse, and in 1935 she gave birth to a daughter, Maia. Picasso was now formally separated from Olga but he could not divorce her, as the financial costs would have been too great.

Large Nude in a Red Armchair, 1929, perhaps reflects the crisis in Picasso's marriage.

Ballplayers on the Beach, 1928, was inspired by beach holidays with Marie-Thérèse.

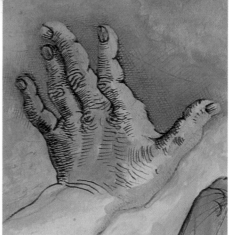

Minotaur and Dead Mare Outside a Cave, painted in 1936.

Picasso has painted the hand in a classical style, but you can see echoes from the artist's Blue Period paintings. This combination of styles helps to create a sinister, dreamlike quality.

TRANSFORMATIONS

Marie-Thérèse reawakened Picasso's drive to be challenging and revolutionary as an artist. Maintaining his interest in Surrealist ideas about dreams, he developed a vision of the human body broken down into strange shapes. Picasso was also working on sculpture with renewed vigor. Helped by a Spanish metal worker named Julio González, he began to produce sculptures made of welded metal rods. This type of sculpture was completely new.

Picasso was also developing another, rather different line of work. He began to make etchings and to design illustrations for books. Etching involves scratching a metal plate with a sharp instrument, which produces a fine line when printed. The result in Picasso's work was both complex and delicate.

During the summer of 1933 he returned to Barcelona. This visit rekindled his earlier interest in bullfighting. Soon he began work on a series of etchings featuring the mythical Minotaur, half man, half bull. According to Greek legend, this monster lived in the labyrinth of King Minos in ancient Crete.

DREAM IMAGES

Many Surrealists painted pictures that sprang entirely from their imagination, and reflected the strange, disconnected world of dreams. Try to paint a picture from your imagination or from a dream you have had. Allow your imagination to take control – remember, this is the world of fantasy. Perhaps you could include mythical beasts or figures, as in the painting below.

GUERNICA

In 1936 Picasso met a young photographer named Dora Maar, who was closely involved with the Surrealists. Graceful, dark-haired, and serious, she became Picasso's new love. The artist's work, meanwhile, had become increasingly tormented, reflecting the distressing events now occurring in Europe, and particularly in Picasso's native Spain.

THE SPANISH CIVIL WAR

In 1936 the Spanish Fascists, led by General Franco, began a rebellion against the elected Republican government of Spain. Spain was split in two, and a cruel and bloody civil war began. The Spanish Fascists were supported by the German Fascists (the Nazis), and in 1937 German airplanes attacked and destroyed the town of Guernica in northeastern Spain. The suffering of the innocent citizens of Guernica shocked the world. Picasso strongly supported the Republicans, and sold paintings to raise money for their cause.

In 1936 Picasso was honored to accept an invitation from the Republicans to become Director of the Prado, the great national art collection in Madrid, Spain. However, he remained in Paris, although many of his friends left France to fight for the cause of the Republicans in Spain. The Spanish Republicans lost the civil war to the Fascists. After 1934 Picasso never returned to Spain.

Guernica, 1937, is a huge mural that pictures the bombing of a Spanish city.

Portrait of a Woman (Dora Maar) was painted in 1942.

IMAGES OF HORROR

In 1937 Picasso was asked by the Republicans to paint a large mural for the Spanish pavilion at the Exposition Universelle in Paris. Picasso chose Guernica as his subject, and in a short space of time produced one the most famous and most powerful paintings in twentieth-century art.

Although it is over 20 feet (6 meters) wide, Picasso painted *Guernica* in just three weeks. To work on a picture of this scale, he took over a large studio in the Rue des Grands-Augustins in Paris (above left). He was assisted by Dora Maar, who filled in some of the painting for him and took photographs of the artist at work.

The painting presents a series of terrifying scenes. It shows the brutality of war and its savage destructiveness. Once, paintings had been used to glamorize war; there is no glamour here, just the grim reality.

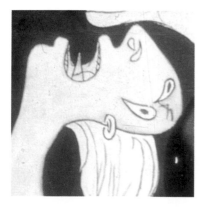

Guernica is an expression of horror at the rise of Fascism. All the figures are victims. The use of black and white and flattened forms increases the power of the stark message.

Later, during World War II, a German officer is said to have visited Picasso in his studio and, seeing *Guernica*, asked, "Did you do this?" Picasso replied, "No. You did." During the late 1930s Picasso made many paintings and drawings that focused on suffering. His work seems to symbolize the atmosphere in Europe at the time, sliding hopelessly into a second world war.

PAINTING MOODS

Experiment with painting different moods – pain, happiness, fear. Concentrate more on the mood you want to convey rather than on a precise image. You could paint a picture to portray a scene from a war. What shapes and colors would best convey the horror and pain of war? Now try painting a completely different mood – a happy holiday, perhaps, or a game. The painting should evoke a sense of joy, relaxation, and fun.

WORLD WAR II

World War II began in 1939. The German Nazis invaded and conquered France and marched into Paris. Picasso could have fled from France, but he decided to stay. He continued to paint and sculpt as best he could throughout the war. Much of his work at this time has a somber, anguished mood, but by staying in Paris, the artist himself became a symbol of freedom.

FRANÇOISE

The Nazis declared that Picasso was a "degenerate" artist. They prevented him from exhibiting his paintings, and it was not easy for him to buy painting materials.

His relationship with Dora Maar had become stale and difficult. In 1943 he met a 21-year-old painter named Françoise Gilot who shared his life for the next ten years.

In 1944 Picasso's wartime work was featured in an exhibition of modern art to celebrate the liberation of Paris. He and Françoise moved to the south of France (known in French as the Midi), and in 1948 they decided to settle there. In 1947 Françoise had given birth to a son, Claude, and in 1949 she had a daughter, Paloma. Picasso enjoyed spending time with his children. For a while, he led the life of a contented family man, painting, sculpting, and designing ceramics.

This somber still life reflects the war years. The candle is a symbol of death. The other features, painted with restraint and simplicity, represent the hardships of life in occupied France.

Pitcher, Candle and Enamel Saucepan, painted in 1945.

Goat's Skull, Bottle and Candle was made between 1951-52.

Most of Picasso's sculpture has a delightful element of surprise. The bottle is a flat sheet, the skull by contrast has been heavily textured, and the horns are bicycle handlebars. The sculpture is cast in bronze.

FOUND OBJECTS

During the war Picasso continued to create sculptures out of things that he had found, which he then had cast in bronze. He made a bull's head out of only a bicycle saddle and a pair of handlebars. Picasso developed an imaginative approach to sculpture and he produced some of the most delightful work of his career.

DESIGN A PLATE

In 1947 Picasso began to work alongside potters at Vallauris, in the south of France. He decorated plates, vases, and other pots with bold designs, especially featuring animals. Try designing your own plate. You can use ordinary, non-shiny, paper plates instead of pottery. Use thick poster paint or acrylic color. Make your designs bold and bright. Start with the outlines – perhaps a fish, a dancer, a face, or just abstract shapes. The outlines may be enough on their own, or you may need to fill them in with color.

THE FINAL YEARS

Picasso's relationship with Françoise Gilot was often difficult. In 1953, when the relationship deteriorated, she left him. Picasso, who was 71, was devastated. No woman had left him before; he had always abandoned them. The following year, however, he met Jacqueline Roque, who later became his second wife.

JACQUELINE

Picasso met Jacqueline at the pottery gallery of Vallauris. She was a young, confident woman, recently divorced. She became Picasso's last, devoted companion, seldom leaving his side. In 1961, after the death of Olga, they were married. Picasso, now 79, was world famous and something of a legend. But it was difficult for him to find any privacy. He complained that he had to barricade himself away to keep the world

out. His final years were spent in grand, secluded houses in the south of France. Isolation and loneliness were the price of the artist's great fame.

Picasso died at the age of 91 in April 1973. He was buried in the grounds of the château he had bought in the south of France. He left behind him a vast private collection of his works, evidence of the huge energy that he had devoted to art throughout his long life.

In 1957 Picasso locked himself away to study Velázquez's *Las Meninas* (above), painted in 1656. He produced 58 pictures on this theme.

Las Meninas, painted in 1957, is a reworking of one of the most famous paintings by the Spanish artist Diego Velázquez.

The Artist and His Model, 1963, one of a series of paintings showing the artist at work.

UNDIMINISHED ENERGY

In this period Picasso devoted a large amount of his time to reworking masterpieces by other painters, such as Velázquez, Delacroix, and Manet. Right up to his death, Picasso was always experimenting, exploring, and creating new ways of expression. His remarkable talent was beyond dispute, and remains a profound influence on twentieth-century art.

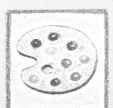

REWORKING GREAT ART

You can see from Picasso's *Las Meninas* (left) that the artist did not simply copy masterpieces. He reworked them in his own style, developing the content in a way that suited him. Try it for yourself. Choose a famous painting that you like, perhaps one of Picasso's from this book. Create your own version of it, or try several versions in different styles. Copy the features that attract you, rework other parts, and invent entirely new elements if you wish.

CHRONOLOGY OF PICASSO'S LIFE

1881 Born on October 25 in Málaga in the south of Spain.

1895 Age 14, entered the School of Fine Arts in Barcelona.

1900 Went to Paris for the first time with Carlos Casagemas.

1901 Casagemas killed himself. Picasso's Blue Period began.

1904 Picasso moved into the Floating Laundry in Paris, where he met Fernande Olivier.

1904-06 Picasso's Rose Period.

1907 Painted *Les Demoiselles d'Avignon*. Met Georges Braque.

1908-14 Cubism began.

1911 Picasso met Eva Gouel Humbert.

1915 Eva died suddenly of tuberculosis.

1917 Went to Rome to design for the ballet *Parade* and met Olga Kokhlova.

1918 Married Olga.

1921 Birth of their son, Paulo.

1925 Involvement with the Surrealists.

1927 Met Marie-Thérèse Walter.

1935 Marie-Thérèse gave birth to Maia. Separated from Olga.

1936 Met the photographer Dora Maar, who became his mistress.

1943 Met Françoise Gilot.

1947 Françoise Gilot gave birth to Claude.

1948 Picasso and Françoise moved to the south of France.

1949 Birth of their daughter, Paloma.

1953 Françoise left Picasso.

1954 Met Jacqueline Roque.

1961 Married Jacqueline.

1973 Died April 8, age 91, at Mougins in the south of France.

A BRIEF HISTORY OF ART

The world's earliest works of art are figurines dating from 30,000 B.C. Cave art developed from 16,000 B.C. In the Classical Age (500-400 B.C.) sculpture flourished in Ancient Greece.

The Renaissance period began in Italy in the 1300s and reached its height in the sixteenth century. Famous Italian artists include Giotto (ca.1266-1337), Leonardo da Vinci (1452-1519), Michelangelo Buonarroti (1475-1564), and Titian (ca.1487-1576).

In Europe during the fifteenth and sixteenth centuries, Hieronymus Bosch (active 1480-1516), Albrecht Dürer (1471-1528), and El Greco (1541-1614) produced great art. Artists of the Baroque period include Peter Paul Rubens (1577-1640) and Rembrandt van Rijn (1606-69).

During the Romantic movement, English artists J.M.W. Turner (1775-1851) and John Constable (1776-1837) produced wonderful landscapes. Diego Velázquez (1599-1660) was a great Spanish artist.

Impressionism began in France in the 1870s. Artists include Claude Monet (1840-1926), Camille Pissarro (1830-1903), and Edgar Degas (1834-1917). Post-Impressionists include Paul Cézanne (1839-1906), Paul Gauguin (1848-1903), and Vincent van Gogh (1853-90).

The twentieth century has seen many movements in art. Georges Braque (1882-1963) painted in the Cubist tradition. Salvador Dali (1904-89) painted in the Surrealist tradition. **Pablo Picasso** (1881-1973) was a prolific Spanish painter at the forefront of modern art. More recently, Jackson Pollock (1912-56) and David Hockney (1937-) have achieved fame.

MUSEUMS AND GALLERIES
The following museums and galleries have examples of Picasso's work:

Musée Picasso, Paris, France
Musée Nationale d'Art Moderne, Paris, France
Museu Picasso, Barcelona, Spain
Prado, Madrid, Spain
National Gallery, London, England
Tate Gallery, London, England
Museum of Modern Art, New York, USA
Metropolitan Museum of Art, New York, USA
Guggenheim Museum, New York, USA
National Gallery, Washington, D.C., USA
Museum of Fine Arts, Boston, USA
Art Institute, Chicago, USA
Philadelphia Museum of Art, USA
Cleveland Museum of Art, USA
Hermitage, St. Petersburg, Russia
Stedelijk Museum, Amsterdam, Netherlands
Kunstmuseum, Basel, Switzerland
Staatsgalerie, Stuttgart, Germany
Neue Pinakothek, Munich, Germany
Queensland Art Gallery, Brisbane, Australia

GLOSSARY
Abstract art Paintings that consist entirely of patterns and shapes, and do not attempt to portray anything in the real world.

Collage The technique of pasting objects or pieces of material onto paper or canvas to create a picture.

Cubism An art movement in which paintings and sculptures are broken up into geometric forms and distorted shapes. The artists used muted colors and showed subjects from more than one angle.

Flat In painting, flat refers to an area covered by a single plain color, without shading or varying tones, which might give the illusion of depth.

Impressionism The name given in the 1870s to a group of artists (Monet, Sisley, Pissarro, and others) who tried to evoke the passing mood of a landscape or scene by working rapidly, using quick brushstrokes.

Post-Impressionism Several artists of the late nineteenth-century, whose work followed closely from that of the Impressionists, are known as Post-Impressionists. They include Cézanne, van Gogh and Gauguin.

Primitive In Picasso's time, ethnic painting and sculpture – from Africa and Polynesia, for example – was referred to admiringly as "primitive" because it was free of the constraints of traditional art.

Surrealism A movement of poets and artists whose work was inspired by their subconscious, dreams, and imagination. They were more interested in the realm of fantasy rather than reality.

INDEX

INDEX OF PICTURES

Special thanks to: The Musée Picasso, Paris. Reunion des Musées Nationaux. Musée National d'Art Moderne, Georges Pompidou Centre, Paris. Tate Gallery Publications, The Tate Gallery, London. The National Gallery, London. The Bridgeman Art Library. Giraudon/Bridgeman Art Library. The National Gallery, Prague. Roger Vlitos. The publishers have made every effort to contact all the relevant copyright holders, and apologize for any omissions that may have inadvertently been made.